# HIGH DAYS
## —AND—
# HOLIDAYS

### CELEBRATING
### THE CHRISTIAN YEAR

DAVID SELF

A LION BOOK
Oxford · Batavia · Sydney

Copyright © 1993 David Self
Line illustrations copyright © 1993 Ivan Hissey

Published by
**Lion Publishing plc**
Sandy Lane West, Oxford, England
ISBN 0 7459 2335 6
**Albatross Books Pty Ltd**
PO Box 320, Sutherland, NSW 2232, Australia
ISBN 0 7324 0597 1

First edition 1993

**Photographs**
J. Allan Cash Photo Library: pages 40, 65, 74, 78, 89; Andes Press Agency: /Carlos Reyes pages 28, 55; Ardea London Ltd: /Jack A. Bailey page 36; Barnaby's Picture Library: pages 42, 57, 62, 79, 86, /Kanus page 38; Christmas Archives: page 26; Nobby Clark: page 27; DLP Photo Library: David Phillips page 15; Ebenezer Pictures: /David Keel page 91, /Eric Marsh page 49, /Christopher Phillips page 64; Sonia Halliday Photographs: pages 11, 58, /Sonia Halliday and Laura Lushington pages 24, 61, 73, /Laura Lushington page 63, /Else Tricket page 85 (above); Institut fur Auslandsbeziehungen, Stuttgart, Germany: page 19; ITC Entertainments Group Ltd: page 14; Lion Publishing: /David Alexander pages 45, 46 (above), 51, 68, 71(above), /Jonathan Roberts page 37, /David Townsend pages 12, 52, 85 (below); Manchester City Council: page 76; Mansell Collection: page 81; Novosti Photo Library (London): /B. Babanov page 66; Rex Features: /Laski page 30, /Alfred page 47, South American Pictures: Marion Morrison page 41; Zefa UK Ltd: pages 17, 23, 34, 70, 82, /Benser page 71 (below), /Janoud page 54, /Mueller page 18, /Norman page 29, /Panda Photo page 33, / Rust pages 20-21.

A catalogue record of this book is available
from the British Library

Printed and bound in Singapore

# CONTENTS

# *I*NTRODUCTION

Think how boring it would be if every day of the year was the same. We would never have anything to look forward to!

Luckily, each year has its special days—important, exciting days. Days that make us impatient while we're waiting for them to arrive but days that are worth waiting for—like the holidays.

For many of us, the best day of the year is our birthday: the day of the year when people give us presents and cards. Husbands and wives like to remember their wedding anniversary: a yearly reminder of the day they were married.

But other special days (or "festivals") are ones we can *all* share.

Different countries have their own festivals but some days, such as Christmas, are celebrated in many countries. And the reason we have Christmas (and lots of other holidays or "holy days" such as Easter) is because of just one man. His name was Jesus.

Christmas, Easter and the other Christian festivals make the year interesting—by giving us days to look forward to. More importantly, as the year goes by, they remind Christians of the main events in the life of Jesus and of what those events mean for us today.

# 1

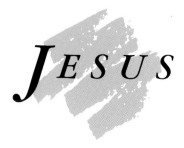

# JESUS

So it all began with Jesus.

But who was Jesus?

For many people, that's the wrong question. We shouldn't be asking "Who was Jesus?" but "Who *is* Jesus?" We shall see why later. But to begin at the beginning...

Jesus was born about two thousand years ago in a little Jewish town called Bethlehem. That wasn't his home, however. That was at Nazareth, seventy miles to the north. Nazareth, like Bethlehem and many other places in the story of Jesus, is still there. It's not far from a large lake called the Sea of Galilee.

## THE FIRST CHRISTMAS

In Nazareth, there lived a carpenter called Joseph and a girl called Mary whom he deeply loved and was soon to marry. One day, Mary saw an angel. The angel told her she was to have a baby. She was to be its mother and the father was to be—no, not Joseph but God himself. And so the baby, whom they were to name Jesus, would be

the Son of God.

That's what Christians believe happened. And that's why, each year, they celebrate the important events of the life of Jesus—because they believe he was so special.

The celebration starts just before Christmas, in part of the year called Advent (see pages 16–19). This is when Christians think of how Mary waited for the birth of Jesus Christ. ("Christ" is not really a name but a title. It means "the anointed one", "the one who will save us".)

After Advent comes Christmas itself (see pages 24–31), which is the birthday of Jesus.

In those days, the country in which Mary and Joseph lived was ruled by the Romans. The Romans wanted to check who should be paying taxes so they held a census—just at the time Jesus was about to be born. This meant that everyone had to go to their home town to have their names put on the tax list.

Although Joseph and Mary lived in Nazareth, Joseph originally came from Bethlehem—so he and Mary had to travel

This stained glass window shows a traditional nativity scene. In the days when few people could read, windows like these were used to teach stories from the Bible.

there for the census. Mary should really have stayed at home because the baby might be born at any time. Even so, she made the journey south, riding on a donkey.

When they got to Bethlehem, the town was so crowded they could not find anywhere to stay. At last, one innkeeper let them stay in the part of his house where the animals were kept. There, in the straw, Mary had her baby. Soon after he had been born, shepherds came down from the nearby hills to worship him.

Some time later, wise and important men from a foreign country also came to visit and worship the child whom they said would be a king. Christians remember this visit on a day now called Epiphany (see pages 32–35).

Forty days after Jesus was born, Mary and Joseph took him to the temple in the capital city of the country, Jerusalem (which was quite near Bethlehem). This was to say "thank you" to God for his safe birth—and it is now marked by the day called Candlemas or "The Presentation of Christ in the Temple" (see pages 36–39).

So far as we know, Jesus spent his boyhood in Nazareth. When he grew up, he worked as a carpenter there—like Joseph. But when he was aged about thirty, everything changed.

## JESUS' WORK BEGINS

His cousin John had become a preacher and was baptizing people in the River Jordan—so he had become known as

The hills and valleys of the land where Jesus travelled and worked.

"John the Baptist". Jesus visited him and was himself baptized in the river. Then Jesus went off to live on his own in the desert for forty days—forty days now remembered in the season of the year called "Lent" (see pages 44–47). This was to give him time to think about the important work he was to do during the next three years of his life.

During this time, with twelve friends or "disciples", he journeyed round the country. He talked or preached to the crowds who came to listen to what he had to say. He taught them how to pray to God. "Call him 'Father' or even 'Daddy'," he said. "And when you pray, say: 'Our Father, who art in heaven...'" And all over the world, people still say the prayer that begins with those words, the "Our Father".

Jesus also taught the people that they should love God—and each other. He told them many stories (called "parables") to remind them of the things they should do—such as caring for those in need or making proper use of the gifts or talents that God had given them. Jesus also healed many people who were ill or in pain.

Then, after three years doing this, Jesus said to his disciples that they should all go to Jerusalem. This was dangerous because many of the Jewish leaders in the city knew how popular Jesus had become and were jealous of him. There was also the danger that the Romans (who were still in control of the country) would arrest him because they thought he might cause trouble—perhaps by trying to make himself ruler of the country.

Even so, Jesus (and his disciples) went to Jerusalem. He entered the city on the

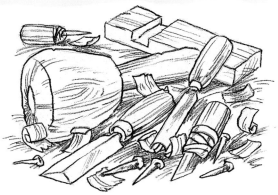

Jesus would have used tools like these when he worked as a carpenter.

first day of the week, Sunday. The crowds cheered him and waved branches from the palm trees—and that day is remembered as Palm Sunday (see pages 52–55).

Jesus spent the next few days, now known as Holy Week (see pages 56–59), teaching in the temple at Jerusalem. But he knew that his enemies would soon arrest him. On the Thursday, he had a last evening meal with his disciples (see pages 57–59) and then went out into a nearby garden to pray.

## JESUS IS BETRAYED

It was one of his own closest friends, a disciple called Judas Iscariot, who betrayed him. Judas had left the meal early and brought soldiers to the garden where Jesus was. Jesus was arrested and taken to the Jewish priests. They accused him of many things. They claimed he was saying things he had no right to say. Things that would make the people disobey the priests. In fact, they felt he was a threat to them and would have liked to have him put to death—but they had not got the power to order this. So, early next morning, they took him to Pontius Pilate. He was the Roman governor of the area (or "province").

## JESUS IS CRUCIFIED

Even though Pilate did not think Jesus was guilty, he knew that the Jewish leaders wanted him killed—and Pilate also knew that the priests had stirred up the crowds against Jesus. If he did not do what the crowds wanted, there might be a riot. So Pilate announced that Jesus was to be put to death by crucifixion that very day—now called Good Friday (see pages 60–63).

**People did not always agree with what Jesus taught; from the film, *Jesus of Nazareth*.**

Jesus was crucified on a large wooden cross just outside the city walls. He died that afternoon and his body was placed in a tomb—which was actually a cave. A huge, heavy stone was used to block the entrance.

But that was not the end of the story. Very early on the next Sunday morning, a friend of Jesus called Mary came to the tomb. The stone had been rolled away and the cave was empty. She fetched the disciples. They too saw what had happened. Later, when Mary was still there (on her own) she saw Jesus. He was alive!

Over the next forty days, Jesus appeared to the other disciples. They were convinced that he had risen from the dead—and was alive again. And this is what all Christians still believe: that death was

Jesus was betrayed by Judas Iscariot and arrested in the Garden of Gethsemane.

not the end of everything for Jesus. Easter is the festival which, each year, recalls this great event (see pages 64–71). What happened afterwards is marked by Ascension Day (see pages 72–75).

## NEW LIFE FOR EVERYONE

Even though Jesus is no longer on earth as a human being, Christians believe that God his Father and he are close to them in a special way, through his Holy Spirit. They think of how this came about at the festival of Pentecost which comes fifty days after Easter (see pages 76–79).

Christians believe that Jesus has proved there is life after death—which is why, as well as saying "Jesus lived ..." they claim that "Jesus *lives*!" What is more, they believe he offers this new, everlasting life to everyone.

So the question isn't "Who was Jesus?" but "Who *is* Jesus?" And for Christians, the answer is, "He is the one who 'saves' us; he is the Christ."

People can talk to God (or pray) at any time and anywhere. Jesus taught his followers the importance of prayer and that they could be sure that God hears all prayers.

# 2

# ADVENT

When is New Year's Day? Most people would say the first of January. But there are lots of different "new year's days"—at different times of the year. In most schools, the "new year" begins when term starts in September or January, when you move to a new class. For some grown-ups in Britain, the fifth of April is an important day because that is the end of the "tax year". For them, the next day is the start of a new tax year in which they have to pay their next lot of taxes to the government. And for Chinese people, New Year's Day comes in late January or early February.

Different religions have their own new year's days as well. For Jews, the new year usually begins in late September. Some Hindus celebrate new year in the autumn, others celebrate it in the spring. But for Christians, the start of the new church year is Advent Sunday. In the West, this is four Sundays before Christmas; and the season of Advent is the time between Advent Sunday and Christmas Day.

The word "Advent" means "coming" or "arrival" and so Advent is a time of waiting for the arrival of Christmas, the coming of Jesus to earth when he was born as a baby at Bethlehem about two thousand years ago. Many of the hymns that are sung in church during this period mention that "coming" of Jesus. Hymns like "O come, O come Emmanuel". "Emmanuel" is an old word meaning "God is with us"—because Christians believe that Jesus is the Son of God.

## GETTING READY

This time of year is a time of great excitement in many ways. People are busy doing their Christmas shopping, buying and sending Christmas cards and decorating their homes. The streets are full of bright lights—and everyone is looking forward to the great festival of Christmas.

So Advent is an exciting time, a time of preparation. But for Christians, there is a much more serious side to it all. Just suppose someone very important was coming to visit you in your home. Think how much you would want to do to get ready for him or her. Tidying up. Putting

Making your own Christmas decorations is more fun than using ones bought in a shop—and they look just as good!

things straight. In the same way, Advent is a time to prepare for the coming of Jesus: to think of the things you have done wrong, and to admit you are sorry for these things. To plan how you can do better in the future ... to put things right for when Jesus comes.

During Advent, some people make or buy Advent calenders as a way of counting the days to Christmas. Usually these calenders have twenty-four "windows". Each of these opens up to show a picture of something linked with this time of year. One may show an angel or one of the shepherds who visited the baby Jesus. Others may show pictures of Christmas presents—and the last window to be opened usually shows Jesus himself, lying in the manger. (There are twenty-four "windows" in an Advent calendar because Advent Sunday usually happens on or near the first of December—and so there are twenty-four days between then and Christmas Day.)

## THE LIGHT OF THE WORLD

In many churches at this time of year there is an Advent wreath (sometimes called an Advent ring or crown). This is a circle made of holly and ivy and in the middle are four candles. They are usually red or purple and each one represents one of the four Sundays of Advent. On Advent Sunday, just one candle is lit. Then, on the second Sunday of Advent, two candles burn brightly—and so on up to the fourth (and last) Sunday of Advent. In some Advent wreaths there is a fifth candle. This extra one is a larger, white one and is lit on Christmas Day itself.

The message of the Advent wreath is that, out of darkness, comes light. Jesus himself said he was "the light of the world"—and so, as Christmas and the coming of Jesus gets nearer and nearer, the greater is the light burning in the darkness of winter.

One exciting place to go Christmas shopping is the *Weihnachtsmarkt* (or Christmas market) in Stuttgart in Germany.

## THE END OF TIME

Carol singing is one way to share the joy of Christmas with others.

But Advent is not just a time to look forward to Christmas. It is a time to look forward to when Jesus will come for a second time. (You can read about Jesus' promise to return in the Bible book of Matthew, chapter 24.) This makes Advent an especially serious time of the year (like Lent). This is because, when Jesus comes again, he will want to know how well we have obeyed his teaching, the teaching he gave during his life on earth.

As we have already said, the Christian year follows the life of Jesus. It begins with Advent Sunday—which, in the Christian church, is "New Year's Day". The most important day of the year will be Easter Sunday, the day on which Jesus came back to life—but before that festival, there are other special days to look forward to. At the end of Advent, there will be Jesus' birthday (Christmas Day). However, before that, in many countries, there is a day set aside to remember St Nicholas.

# 3

# *S*T NICHOLAS

(6 DECEMBER)

All Dutch children know that St Nicholas (or "Sinterklaas" as they often call him) lives in Spain. And they know that, each year, in the early days of December he and his friend, Peter, come to visit the Netherlands. That's why they sing:

---

*Look, there is the steamer from*
*faraway lands,*
*It brings us St Nicholas; he's waving*
*his hands,*
*His horse is a-prancing on deck,*
*up and down,*
*The banners are waving in village*
*and town.*

---

And that's what happens each December in Amsterdam and in other places in the Netherlands. St Nicholas arrives, wearing a bishop's robe and, on his

Father Christmas (or Santa Claus) doesn't visit only cold, snowy countries in a sleigh drawn by reindeer. In Mombasa, Kenya, Christmas is warm and sunny, and Father Christmas travels by donkey!

head, a mitre. He has a white beard, white gloves—and a white horse. And, seated on his horse, he rides round the city with Peter walking at his side. The people cheer, the church bells ring and there's often a band leading the procession with policemen on motorbikes, their lights flashing. And later on, so young Dutch children believe, St Nicholas and Peter will visit every child who's been well behaved during the last year and leave him or her a present.

It's a nice idea.

In fact, the *real* St Nicholas lived hundreds of years ago—and not in Spain but in a place called Myra—which is on the southern coast of what is now called Turkey. Indeed, Nicholas was Bishop of Myra.

He was very rich. He was very generous—and he was very shy. So, although he liked helping people and giving them presents, he never wanted people to thank him. He liked doing good *secretly.*

## THE SECRET HELPER

One well-known story tells of the day when Bishop Nicholas accidentally overheard three young women quarrelling about something not being fair. It seemed they were grumbling about being poor, so poor that nobody would marry them. And then Nicholas heard their father join them and say how sorry he was that he had no job and little hope of earning any money to pay for their weddings. While they were still talking, Nicholas tip-toed away.

That night, Nicholas returned to their house and threw a large bag of gold coins in through an open window. "This is the best way," he said to himself. "If I give them money in an obvious way, I might upset them."

Bishop Nicholas hoped that no one would see him throw the bag of coins through an open window.

Next morning, the father and his daughters awoke and when they got up, yes, they found the bag of gold.

"Well," said the father. "Now my eldest daughter can get married!"

And that's what happened. A handsome young man fell in love with her, the father paid for a splendid wedding and all was well.

Except that the other two daughters were still unhappy. And Nicholas overheard *their* grumbles. So that night, just as before, he threw a bag of gold in through the open window. And again, just as before, the following morning they found the gold. As you can guess, it wasn't long before the second daughter was married.

Some days after that, Nicholas was again passing the same house. The father and youngest daughter were sitting together quietly and sadly—because there was no

money for a third wedding. Nicholas went on his way.

And later that night, back he came to leave a third bag of gold—but this time the father heard him and came to the door. Nicholas tried to get away, but the father caught him by the arm. "I've been wondering who had been leaving the bags of gold and now I see it's you, Bishop Nicholas."

Nicholas tried to stop him. "I don't want any thanks, I don't want any fuss . . ."

The father tried very hard to thank Bishop Nicholas but Nicholas said he should not thank him but give thanks to God who had given Nicholas money to use well. And so the two men gave each other a hug of friendship and Nicholas went on his way. Soon afterwards, the third daughter was married.

So that's why some people believe St Nicholas goes round giving presents to those who deserve them.

On the night before Christmas... in some countries, children hang up a stocking on Christmas Eve, hoping that Santa Claus will fill it with presents.

### A NEW NAME

And when some Dutch people moved away from the Netherlands to live in the United States of America, they carried on the custom, only this time St Nicholas (in his red bishop's robe and with his white beard) arrived in New York and went round *that* city, giving out presents. The other people who lived there saw what was happening and liked the idea. But when they heard the Dutch people calling him "Sinterklaas", they thought they were saying "Santa Claus". And so lots of people started talking about "Santa Claus"— the man who comes just before Christmas to give presents to everyone who's been good.

# 4

# *C*HRISTMAS EVE

( 2 4 D E C E M B E R )

He was twenty-four when everything changed. Up till then he'd been known as Francesco Bernardone. He lived in what is now Italy. He was the son of rich parents who had let him grow up having exactly what he wanted and doing exactly what he pleased. He wore the most fashionable clothes, he spent money without a care in the world. Indeed, he thought only of enjoying himself; of doing just what he wanted with no regard for anyone else. Until that year. The year 1206.

Then St Francis (as we now remember him) suddenly began to realize how selfish he was being. He started to think of the poor, of people who were suffering or ill. He gave away all his possessions, even the

St Francis is best-known for his love of birds and animals, but he also made the first "Christmas crib".

clothes he was wearing. He lived simply, owning nothing and eating only what he could beg or was given. Others joined him in his new way of life. They called each other "Brother" and eventually they became known as Franciscans. These "brothers", or "friars", as they were also known, followed a strict "rule" or way of life.

Francis knew Christmas was a most important festival and one particular Christmas (in the year 1223) was to become a very special one—and not just for him.

As they climbed the hillside, people must have wondered what Francis wanted to show them.

## A SECRET PLAN

That winter, Francis visited some of his brother friars who lived at a village called Greccio which is high up a river valley near the ancient city of Rieti. He was trying to find peace and quiet and to imagine the life Jesus must have led. Midway through December he had an idea. He sent for one of the older friars called John.

"You wanted to see me?"

"Brother John, yes. Yes, I did."

"For what reason?"

"You know it's nearly Christmas?"

"Of course. Why..." Suddenly John looked anxious. "You *are* going to spend Christmas with us? Here at Greccio?"

"Oh yes. Yes, I shall spend Christmas here. But I've been thinking about that first Christmas. I want to make a picture of how it was. I want the people, all the people who live around here, to *understand.* To understand what it was like. How the Child of Bethlehem suffered hardships for us. Came to earth. Was born. Lay in a manger. Perhaps in a stable."

No one else knew what Francis and John were planning. Secretly, John made all the necessary arrangements. Up in a cave, on the hillside near Greccio, John placed a manger, full of hay. He arranged also for there to be an ox and an ass standing by.

When Christmas Eve came, Francis asked the people of the district each to bring a lighted candle and come with him to the cave. And so they did, taking care to see that their candles did not blow out as they climbed up the mountain path. From all along the valley they came, wondering why Francis had asked them.

They soon found out.

## THE FIRST "CHRISTMAS CRIB"

There, at the entrance to the cave was the manger, and around it people dressed up to represent Mary and Joseph and the shepherds.

"That's how it must have been when Jesus was born!" said the people. Francis was delighted. "Greccio is a new Bethlehem," he said. "This is to remind us that Jesus was born in a simple stable, surrounded by animals. Worshipped by ordinary shepherds. Visited by wise men."

And there, by that manger, the first "Christmas crib" scene, a holy communion service was held by a priest with Francis helping him and singing the gospel story of how Jesus was born at Bethlehem in Judea. Today there is a convent at Greccio where followers of St Francis still live and there, each Christmas Eve, the birth of Jesus is remembered in the same way. Nowadays, Christians all over the world act out that scene at Christmas. The performances are called "Nativity Plays"—because "nativity" means "birth".

live among us, in a most humble way.

Besides making models of the crib scene or arranging Nativity Plays, many Christians go to church late on Christmas Eve to take part in a midnight service. Often, this is a holy communion service (just like the one celebrated in the village of Greccio) and it may then be called "Midnight Mass". The word "mass", used

One of the shepherds visits Mary and the baby Jesus in this modern production of a nativity play.

## BIRTHDAY CELEBRATIONS

And in thousands of churches all around the world (as well as in schools and homes and many other places) people make a "crib" or model of the Christmas scene—with the baby Jesus lying in a straw-filled manger in the stable. It is a reminder that, although Jesus was so "special", he came to earth to

This colourful crib scene from Peru includes both traditional characters from the Christmas story and figures from everyday life.

by Catholic Christians, comes from a Latin word *missa* which occurs in the service. But for all Christians, the Christmas crib and midnight service are reminders of how Jesus came to earth and was born as a baby on that very first Christmas two thousand years ago.

# 5

# CHRISTMAS DAY

## (25 DECEMBER)

"I'm dreaming of a white Christmas" is the start of a very popular song—and people who live in northern Europe and North America often wonder if it will snow at Christmas and they'll wake up that morning and find everywhere white and sparkling—just as it is on so many Christmas cards!

One thing is certain about the first Christmas Day when Jesus was born in Bethlehem: it *wasn't* snowing then! We know this because there were shepherds

with their flocks of sheep up in the hills that night. (You can read about these shepherds who saw angels telling them to go and worship the baby Jesus in the Bible book of Luke, chapter 2). If it *had* been cold and snowy, they would have had their sheep and young lambs down in the valley or indoors!

## WHY DECEMBER 25?

In fact, we don't know for certain at what time of the year Jesus was born. When Matthew and Luke came to write down their stories of how he was born (the stories we now find in the Bible) neither of them thought to say what time of year it was. But three hundred or more years after Jesus was born, Christians began to think it would be a good idea to have one special day in the year when they could all remember his birthday. But why choose 25 December? (In Eastern Europe, many Orthodox Christians begin their Christmas celebrations on 6 January.)

One good reason the early Christians had for selecting 25 December as Christmas Day was that it already was a feast right across the Roman Empire. In Latin (the language of the Romans), it was called "Dies Natalis Invicti Solis"—which means "The Birthday of the Unconquered Sun". It was a feast to celebrate the fact that

*Opposite.* In many countries children perform nativity plays at Christmas. Here some excited "shepherds" are waiting to play their part.

the shortest day of the winter was over, the days would now get longer and longer and the sun (instead of being "conquered" by the cold of winter) would get stronger and stronger as another summer approached.

And, because Jesus brought such good news for all people, he was a kind of new "sun" or light coming into the world. So that old Roman festival became his birthday.

## CHRISTMAS CELEBRATIONS

To celebrate his birthday, many people decorate their homes with holly and Christmas trees. Both of these are "evergreens"; plants which do not lose their leaves in winter—another sign of life in the darkness of winter. Nowadays, people decorate Christmas trees with electric lights. In olden times they used to use candles—which was very dangerous as the tree could catch fire! But both candles and modern electric lights can be reminders that Jesus is the "light" of the world.

Many Christians go to church on Christmas morning. The church building will also be decorated cheerfully with candles and perhaps a Christmas tree. And often there is a crib showing the scene in Bethlehem. Because it's such a happy day, everyone is very cheerful, wishing each other "Merry Christmas". When the service begins, everyone joins in popular

Though their homes have been destroyed by an earthquake, these children are able to celebrate Christmas with a Christmas tree provided by relief workers.

Christmas carols or songs such as: "Once in royal David's city stood a lowly cattle shed", "Hark! the herald angels sing" and "O come, all ye faithful". This last one has a special verse for singing on Christmas morning. It begins:

*Yes, Lord we greet Thee,*
*Born this happy morning;*
*Jesu, to Thee be glory given ...*

After church, families go back home to give and receive presents (if they have not already done so) and then to get ready for Christmas dinner. In many countries these days the main course is roast turkey. This was not always the case, because in olden days there used not to be any turkeys in European countries. In those times, people used to have pork or a roast goose—or even roast peacock! In Britain, the main course may be followed by Christmas pudding and mince pies. This custom goes back several hundred years to the time when there was no fresh fruit to be had at this season of the year and when sugar was too expensive for ordinary people to use much. So then people used to make their special puddings out of spices and dried fruits (like raisins) and nuts—the same sort of things a Christmas pudding is made from today.

None of this may seem to have very much to do with a baby being born into a family who lived two thousand years ago—especially a family who were not very well off and who could not find an inn with any room where they could stay. But it was still an important and happy day. And because Christmas Day is now remembered as the birthday of Jesus, it is right that it too should be a happy day and celebrated with presents and parties—even with a birthday (or Christmas) cake!

Traditional Christmas foods include Stollen and shaped cookies (Germany) and mince pies (Great Britain).

## THE CHRISTMAS MESSAGE

But Christians also remember what they believe is the true message of Christmas. And the message is that, in a very special way, God became a person by being born to Mary. God himself became a little child—not in a palace but in a humble animal shelter. He grew up, like us. He did many good deeds. Even so, he suffered terribly at the hands of evil people, but he did it all to bring life and hope to the whole world. So it's right to share in Jesus Christ's festival day or birthday. In Britain, in olden times the word "Mass" was used to mean "a festival day" (as well as a church service). And so 25 December (or Christ's Festival Day) came to be called "Christ's-mass Day".

# 6

# $E$ *PIPHANY*

(6 JANUARY)

She is old, she wears tattered, shabby clothes, she is called "la Befana"—and she's a kind of good fairy. In Italy, many children believe that she visits their homes on "Twelfth Night" (the twelfth night after the birth of Jesus, which is 5 January). If the children have been good (so the story goes), she will leave them presents of toys or sweets. If they have been naughty, all she will leave them is a lump of coal or a heap of dust!

So before they go to bed, they hang up a stocking—hoping, of course, that next morning they will find something pleasant in it! Often, a grown-up will dress up and pretend to be la Befana—and when Italian children see this person they call out, "Ecco la Befana!" ("Here comes la Befana!")

La Befana's name comes from the word "Epiphany" which in turn comes from a Greek word meaning "appearance" or "showing". The feast of Epiphany (which happens the day after Twelfth Night) is the time when Christians remember how the wise men came to visit the baby Jesus at Bethlehem. They were the first people from another country to see him and so Epiphany got its name as the day on which Jesus was "shown" to non-Jewish people. Their visit was a sign that, when he grew up, his message was to be for all the peoples of the world and not just for those who lived in his own country.

## FOLLOWING A STAR

The Bible tells us very little about the wise men or the "magi" as they are sometimes called. All we know for sure is that they came from the East, following a bright star which seemed to lead them to Jerusalem.

Once they arrived there, they went to King Herod. (You can read about this in the Bible book of Matthew, chapter 2.)

"Where is he who is born king of the Jews?" they asked. "We have seen his star and have come to worship him."

This angered Herod (because of course he thought *he* was king of the Jews) but he said nothing. Instead, he called all the priests and wise men of Jerusalem together and asked them what they thought. They told him how prophets or teachers in times long ago had said that, one day, a king

In Germany, these children act out the coming of the wise men to the baby Jesus at Epiphany.

would be born in the little town of Bethlehem. So Herod spoke privately to the wise men, telling them to go and find the new king and then come back to him and tell him what they had found out.

The star then led the wise men to the baby Jesus at Bethlehem, and there they gave him presents: gold, pure incense called frankincense (which makes a sweet-smelling smoke and is still used in some

33

The wise men brought gifts of gold, frankincense and myrrh.

## WHO WERE THE WISE MEN?

That really is all we know about them. We do not even know there were three of them: we have just guessed that must be so because they brought three presents. Nor do we know if, as some people say, they themselves were kings. Perhaps they were—which is why we sing Christmas carols like "We three kings of Orient are" (the Orient being another word for the East). In some stories about them we are told that their names were Melchior, Caspar and Balthazar—but even that is not certain.

churches) and a kind of precious ointment called myrrh.

But then the wise men were warned in a dream that Herod would harm the baby Jesus if he found him—so they left the country "by another way".

What is certain is that their presents had special meanings. Gold was a sign that Jesus was to be a very special king. Frankincense was a sign that he was from God—and myrrh (which was used when people died) was a sign that he was to suffer for his friends and followers.

## OTHER GIFT BRINGERS

So it is not until Epiphany that some people put the figures of the wise men in the crib scenes they arrange at home or in church—and because the wise men brought gifts, Epiphany (as well as Christmas) has become a time for giving presents. In Britain, long ago, rich people gave presents of gold, frankincense and myrrh to the church. The Queen still does this at a royal chapel in St James's Palace in London. The gold is later changed into money and given to poor people, the frankincense is used in church and the myrrh is given to a hospital.

And in Italy at this time, la Befana brings presents for children. But what has she to do with Epiphany (apart from her name)? The stories told about her say that she was sweeping her house when the wise men went past on their way to see Jesus. She was too busy to pay any attention to them but said she would see them on their way back. But then, of course, they went home another way—and so she never saw them. Ever since, she has been trying to make up for this by giving people presents herself.

In Russia, they tell a similar story about an old woman called Baboushka. In this tale, the wise men visited Baboushka (who lived all alone in a forest) on Christmas Eve. They asked her to travel with them to see the new-born king, and she said she would follow the next day. But by then, she did not know which way to go. Since then, so the story goes, she has journeyed through the countryside every Christmas—giving presents to children, rather like a "Mother Christmas".

# 7

# *C*ANDLEMAS

(2 FEBRUARY)

When does Christmas end? Most people say on Twelfth Night—that is, on the evening of 5 January, the twelfth day after Christmas. But in olden times, many people used to say that the Christmas season lasted for forty days—until the second day of February which was called Candlemas. They also thought this was the

The badger is one of the animals linked with Candlemas folklore.

day that decided what sort of weather there would be for the rest of the winter. If Candlemas Day was sunny and fine (so they said) there would be bad weather to come—but if Candlemas Day was wet and cold, then the worst of the winter was over.

They used to tell a similar story in Germany. "On Candlemas Day, the badger always wakes up from his winter sleep and peeps out of his hole. If he finds it is snowy, he decides it is time to end his sleep (or hibernation) because he knows that winter is nearly over. But if he finds the sun is shining on that day, then he goes back into his hole for he knows there will be more wintry weather yet to come." The story is much the same in the United States of America, where a ground hog (or woodchuck) rather than a badger forecasts the weather.

## LIGHT IN THE DARKNESS

But how did this particular day come to be called *Candlemas*? The answer is that it was the day of the year when all the candles

Today, candles may be used to remind people of Jesus, "the Light of the World".

that were to be used in the church during the coming year were brought into church and a blessing was said over them—so it was the Festival Day (or "mass") of the Candles.

Candles were important in those days not only because there was no electric light. Some people thought they gave protection against plague and illness and famine. For Christians, they were (and still are) a reminder of something even more important. Before Jesus came to earth, it was as if everyone was "in the dark". People often felt lost and lonely. Afraid. As if they were on their own, with no one to help them. Then came Jesus with his message that he is with his followers always ready to help and comfort them. As if he is a guiding light to them in the darkness.

(You can read about this in the Bible book of John, chapter 8:12.) So Christians often talk of Jesus as "the Light of the World"—and candles are lit during church services as a reminder of this.

## BLESSING THE BIRTH

Candlemas Day has two other names. One is the "Presentation of Christ in the Temple". The other is the "Purification of the Blessed Virgin Mary". Both these names come from one special event in the life of the baby Jesus.

Forty days after a Jewish boy was born, it was the custom for his parents to take him to the temple in Jerusalem (if they possibly could) to "present" or show him to God as a way of saying thank you for his safe birth. There was also a service of purification or blessing for his mother—so we get these two names for the day on which we remember these events in Jesus' life. Nowadays, most Christians call the day the "Presentation of Christ in the Temple".

When Mary and Joseph took Jesus to the Temple, they met two very, very old, holy people there. One was called Anna, the other Simeon. When Simeon saw the baby

**Candles are often used by Christians as a symbol of their prayers.**

Jesus he knew he was a very special child. Simeon was so happy to have lived long enough to see Jesus that he said he was now happy to die. The words he then said have been remembered by Christians who sometimes sing them in church. "Lord, now you let your servant depart in peace," he said—and he went on to describe Jesus as a "light" to brighten the lives of all people. (You can read about this in the Bible book of Luke, chapter 2.) And that, of course, is another reason for lighting candles on this day.

One particular thing people used to do on this day was to light a special candle in the evening and then sit around talking and drinking a kind of hot wine called punch—and, as a treat, children were allowed to stay up for as long as the candle burned!

## A SPECIAL MOTHER

This is just one of several days in the year when Christians remember Mary, the mother of Jesus. Some Christians do this more than others. There are those who say that it is wrong to pay too much attention to her because all their respect should be given to Jesus. Other Christians say that, because Jesus is so important, it is right also to respect his mother. So they remember her on this day—and on other days such as 25 March.

This date is exactly nine months before Christmas Day and is called the Feast of the Annunciation. It is a time for remembering how the Angel Gabriel appeared to Mary and told her (or *announced* to her) that she was to have a baby called Jesus.

We know little about the later years of Mary's life—except that she was present at the crucifixion of Jesus and that she was in Jerusalem at the time of the first Pentecost. But one other day of the year on which Mary is remembered is 15 August—Assumption Day. This recalls a story which says that, at the end of her earthly life, Mary was taken up (or *assumed*) into heaven. Because Mary is especially important to Roman Catholic Christians, this day is a holiday in many Catholic countries.

Simeon was overjoyed when he recognized the baby Jesus as the person God had promised to send to rescue his people.

# 8

# *SHROVE TUESDAY*

Pancakes and processions, feasting and football... Shrove Tuesday or "Mardi Gras" is celebrated in all sorts of ways. In some countries it's just called "Carnival". But whatever it's called and however it's celebrated, it's a time for enjoying your-self—before the much more sober period called Lent which begins the following day, Ash Wednesday.

In Britain it's called Shrove Tuesday. The word "Shrove" comes from an old medieval word, "shriven". This means to be forgiven your sins, the things you have done wrong. Some people (though not as many as used to) go to church on this day to tell God how sorry they are for the mean and selfish things they have done in the last year. So the day came to be called "Shrove Tuesday".

In some countries (especially ones in which they speak French) this day is called "Mardi Gras". This means "Fat Tuesday". Not because the day is "fat" but because, during Lent, people used not to eat any meat or dairy produce. So, on "Fat Tuesday", they ate up everything that contained any meat or fat. In fact, they ate up any food which would not last the forty days of Lent in those time before freezers or refrigerators. So "Fat Tuesday" came to be a great day for feasting.

## ANCIENT TRADITIONS

In Britain, people got into the habit of using up any cooking fat and their eggs and milk (which are both dairy products) by making pancakes. Even today, many families have fun on Shrove Tuesday (or

"Pancake Day") frying and tossing pancakes. In some towns and villages, they hold pancake races. A bell is rung and then the contestants run along the main street, tossing pancakes in a frying pan as they go. One place where this still happens is Olney in England: for over five hundred years there has been a pancake race there, from the market square to the parish church.

In many towns, there used to be a match, something like a game of soccer, on Shrove Tuesday. All the men and boys of the town used to take part—and there weren't many rules! They didn't play on a pitch and the goals might be three miles apart! All you had to do was to get the ball into the other team's goal using any method you liked: carrying it, fighting the other team, even pushing your opponents into any handy river! In one place where they still play this kind of "wide football", they have made one rule. The ball mustn't be carried by motorbike, car or helicopter!

## CARNIVAL TIME

The celebrations vary from country to country. In Germany, the day is called "Fasching". There is a great deal of feasting

Fancy dress parades like this one in Rio, Brazil, are part of the "Mardi Gras" celebrations in many countries.

In German-speaking countries people dress up and wear masks at the time of feasting and fun known as *Fasching*.

and drinking; people wear fancy dress and masks and go to parties or join in street parades. In Italy, as well, there are processions and pageants at this time of year, especially in Venice and a town called Viareggio, when many people wear elaborate costumes. This time of the year is called "carnevale". The "carne" part of this Italian word means "meat"; "vale" is farewell or goodbye—so "carnival" means "Goodbye to meat" until Lent is over!

Probably the biggest carnival processions take place in Rio de Janeiro in Brazil where they last for three days. Different groups (called "schools") take part and each group spends a great deal of money on costumes and on the decorated floats which take part in the various processions. And all the time the music of a dance called the samba can be heard. For the people of Rio, many of whom are very poor indeed, carnival is a time to forget their problems.

Carnival also happens in the West Indies—especially on the island of Trinidad. People prepare for this event from the beginning of the year. They make elaborate costumes and compose special songs or calypsos. Each year, one calypso is selected as that year's carnival song.

The carnival itself lasts for two days. It begins very early on the Monday before Mardi Gras and the start of carnival is called "Jouvay" (which comes from the French words, "Le jour est ouvert"—meaning "The day is open"). On Tuesday, Mardi Gras, people appear on the streets in their special costumes; the steel bands play; there are many, many fireworks and the singing and dancing continues until midnight. Then the carnival is over; it really is "farewell to meat" for now it is the first day of Lent, Ash Wednesday.

# 9

# *A*SH WEDNESDAY AND LENT

"Wearing sackcloth and ashes" used to mean what it says. Long ago, when you wanted to show how very sorry you were about something you'd done wrong, then you went around wearing sackcloth and you covered yourself in ashes!

Nobody does that now—except that, on Ash Wednesday (the first day of Lent), some Christians have a tiny smudge of ashes put on their foreheads as a sign of sorrow at not having been good over the last year.

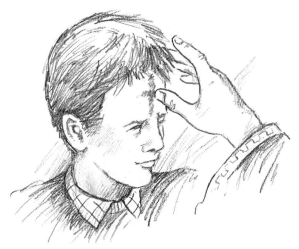

In churches where this happens, the priest first burns the palm crosses that have been kept from last year's Palm Sunday (see page 55) and then mixes the ashes of these crosses with holy water (which has been blessed) to make a kind of greyish paste. Then, when people go to church on Ash Wednesday, the priest dips his thumb in the paste and uses it to make the sign of the cross on each person's forehead.

### A TIME TO THINK

Lent is a serious time of year for Christians. It is a time when they think not just about what they have done wrong in the past but how they could be better in the future. It lasts forty days—from Ash Wednesday to the Saturday just before Easter Sunday—which is sometimes called Holy Saturday. (The Sundays in Lent do not count towards the forty days.)

For Christians, the forty days of Lent are a time of preparation and of thinking ahead to the excitement of Easter. They also remind Christians of the forty days Jesus spent in the wilderness or desert. This happened when he was about thirty and just before he started his work of teaching and healing people.

## JESUS IS TEMPTED

At this time Jesus was baptized in the River Jordan by John the Baptist. Then Jesus went into the wilderness—all on his own— to think about the work that lay ahead of him. And during the time he spent in this desert place, he "fasted". That is, he went without food.

Not surprisingly, he was tempted to use the great power he had been given by God to perform miracles. First, the devil put this idea into his head: "If you really are the Son of God, then you can make all these stones into loaves of bread. So why don't you?" (You can read about this in the Bible book of Matthew, chapter 4.)

But even though Jesus was very hungry, he did not give in. He knew he was being tested. So he did not give way to temptation, but answered the devil by saying, "Man does not live just by eating bread but by listening to what God tells us is right."

Then the devil took Jesus to the top of the great temple in the holy city of

Perhaps it was near here that Jesus came to be baptized by his cousin, John, in the River Jordan. Immediately after the excitement of his baptism, Jesus faced one of his hardest tests.

It was in desert country like this that Jesus fasted and prayed for forty days, facing decisions about his life and work.

Jerusalem. "Look," said the devil. "If you really *are* God's son, throw yourself down to the ground—because surely God will send his angels to catch you and stop you hurting yourself. And think how that would impress people."

But again Jesus did not give in to the temptation. "I tell you," he said to the devil, "it is written that you must not try to tempt God or try to test him to prove his power."

Even so, the devil tried a third time to tempt Jesus. This time he made Jesus look at all the countries of the world, as if he were seeing them from the top of a very high mountain. And the devil put a thought into the mind of Jesus. "I will give you all these countries to rule over—if you will kneel down and worship me. Just think how powerful you could be!"

But again Jesus overcame the temptation. "Away with you," he said. "You must worship only God and no one else."

So then the devil knew that he was beaten and for a time he stopped tempting Jesus.

Jesus was now even stronger in his mind; he could say "no" to what he knew was wrong. And that is one of the things that Christians hope that they can learn during the forty days of Lent each year: to say "no" to what is wrong.

## FASTING AND SHARING

In olden times, people used to fast during Lent—just like Jesus did in the wilderness. They did not go without all food—but many of them gave up eating meat and rich food (which is why Shrove Tuesday is a day for eating everything up!). In some churches, especially in Russia and Greece, Lent is called the Great Fast.

Nowadays Christians do not fast in the same way but many of them do try to give up some food or activity for Lent. Some grown-ups give up alcohol. Others give up eating something such as chocolates or sweets. This is partly to prove to themselves that their minds can "control" their bodies and that they don't *have* to have a drink or a sweet every time they think they'd like one! And some Christians use the money they save by not buying drinks or sweets to give to poor or really hungry people.

But, more importantly, this is also a way to remember how Jesus was tempted and

Hungry refugees reach out eagerly as relief workers hand out bread... During Lent, many Christians give money to charities which help the hungry and homeless.

continued to rely on God. And, just as Jesus let himself be "tested" in the wilderness, so Christians try to use the forty days of Lent as a period to strengthen *them*selves.

# 1 0

# *MOTHERING SUNDAY*

The Sunday in the middle of Lent has many names: Mid-Lent Sunday, Refreshment Sunday, (because people used to have a bit of a feast on this day, to celebrate having got half way through their Lenten fast!) Simnel Sunday and even "Laetare" Sunday. In Britain, most people know the fourth Sunday in Lent as Mothering Sunday. One name it *shouldn't* be called is Mother's Day—which is another day altogether.

## MOTHER'S DAY

The first **Mother's Day** happened in 1907. It was started by an American woman named Anna Jarvis who lived in the city of Philadelphia. He mother had recently died and she felt that one day in the year should be set aside on which people could think about their mothers and all that they had meant to them.

The idea became popular. In 1914, the American government made it official and since then the second Sunday in May has been called Mother's Day. And, on that day in the United States of America, Canada, Australia, and many other countries, people give presents to their mothers. Some wear a carnation: a red carnation as a sign of thanks for a person who is alive, a white carnation in memory of anyone who has died.

But that, of course, is later in the year than **Mothering Sunday**.

## THE MOTHER CHURCH

No one is absolutely certain exactly how the idea of Mothering Sunday began, but we know that on this day, three or four hundred years ago, people who lived in little villages made a point of going not to their local church but to the nearest big church. To what was called the Mother Church. And some would go to the nearest city to worship in the cathedral. (A cathedral is a very large church and the "mother church" of all other churches in that area or "diocese".)

So Mothering Sunday is a day on which Christians give thanks for "Mother Church".

Giving your mother flowers is a special part of Mother's Day and Mothering Sunday.

## GIVING PRESENTS

For a long time, it has also been a day for giving thanks for all the things our mothers do for us. Years ago, many young girls "went into service". That meant that they left home to go and work as maids or servants in the houses of wealthy families. Many boys also had to leave home to find work. Often they became "apprentices". This meant they stayed with a skilled worker, learning his trade or skill.

In those days, there were no real holidays and servants and apprentices were given very little free time. But on Mid-Lent Sunday, they were given time off to go home to visit their mothers. Some of the maids were given a special cake to take as a present to their mothers and some of the boys used to gather a bunch of spring flowers on their way home— also as a present for Mother!

The special kind of cake often eaten on this day is called Simnel cake. It's still made in many parts of England, though its shape varies from place to place. In one town called Devizes, it's baked in the

Housemaids in their "Sunday best" and laden with gifts set off to visit their mothers.

shape of a star. In another, it's a flat, round shape. Simnel cake is always very spicy and usually covered with almond paste or thick marzipan. In Shrewsbury, they eat Simnel cake at Easter and there they often put eleven or twelve marzipan eggs on top of the cake. Each egg was traditionally meant to represent one month that the boy or girl who gave the cake to his or her mother had been away from home.

## A DAY FOR REJOICING

A Latin name for this Sunday is Laetare Sunday. "Laetare" means "rejoice". On this day services in Roman Catholic churches begin with these words from the Bible: "Rejoice ye with Jerusalem and be glad with her . . ." So, in the days when the service was in Latin, the service on this Sunday began, "Laetare . . ." But why "rejoice" in the middle of Lent? Simply because Easter is getting closer and closer. Soon the time of fasting will be over and there will be all the excitement of Easter Day.

On Laetare Sunday the Pope blesses a special ornament called the Golden Rose. It is made in the shape of a bunch of roses and it is given to a person or group of people who have done something to help the Catholic Church.

In many churches, children are given a small bunch or posy of flowers (perhaps violets or primroses) which they can give to their mothers. And lots of people give cards or other presents (such as boxes of chocolates) as a way of saying "thank you" to their mothers. However it is marked, Mothering Sunday is a day for being grateful and thinking of what other people do for us—and for being grateful to "Mother Church" and all *it* means to those who go there week by week.

# 11

# PALM SUNDAY

What has a wooden donkey on wheels got to do with the most holy week of the year? The answer can be found in some German towns and villages on the day of the year called Palm Sunday, the first day of Holy Week and the Sunday before Easter Day.

The donkey is still used for transport in rural parts of the Holy Land.

On this day, Christians remember how Jesus was cheered by the crowds as he rode into Jerusalem, on a donkey. So, in Germany, people recall this event by pulling a carved, wooden figure of Jesus seated on a wooden donkey (called a "Palmesel") in a procession. In some Alpine villages, this procession begins on a nearby hilltop (just as Jesus began his journey on a hill outside Jerusalem) and then everyone makes their way to the church in the middle of the town.

## RIDING ON A DONKEY

Jesus had spent three years journeying round Palestine, teaching and healing people. Then came the time when he knew he had to return to the capital city, Jerusalem. When he and his closest friends (or disciples) came near to Jerusalem, they stopped at a place near a hill called the Mount of Olives. Jesus sent two of his disciples into a nearby village. "There you will find a donkey," he said. "Bring it to me. And if anyone asks what

On the first Palm Sunday the crowds welcomed Jesus as he rode into Jerusalem on a donkey.

you are doing, tell them that the Lord has need of it."

So that is what they did. They went to the village and found a donkey tied up in the street. They started to untie it and, as they did, people who were standing around there asked them what they thought they were doing. The disciples told them what Jesus had said—and the people let them lead the donkey away. (You can read about this in the Bible book of Matthew, chapter 21.)

When they had brought it to Jesus, they put their cloaks on it and Jesus sat on it. And so he rode into Jerusalem, seated not like some important ruler or king might have been—proudly on a great white horse—but seated humbly on a simple donkey such as all the ordinary people used in that country. Even so, crowds of people flocked to see him, lining the road

to get a good view and to cheer the man they had heard so much about. They felt he was so important that they put their cloaks on the roadway or tore down branches from the nearby palm trees and put them on the road—so that there was a sort of carpet for the donkey to walk along. And all the people cried out, "Hosanna, hosanna!"—which means, "Save us, we pray". (They shouted this because they hoped Jesus would free them from the Romans who had taken over their country and who were ruling it strictly.)

## PALM CROSSES AND PRAYERS

Not just in Germany but in many other countries, people act out what happened that very first Palm Sunday. In Jerusalem itself, for hundreds of years, there has been

These people have recaptured something of the excitement of the first Palm Sunday,
waving palm branches as they walk through the streets of Ayacucho in Peru.

a procession from the Mount of Olives to a church in the middle of Jerusalem. And in many countries, churches are decorated with big palm branches. During some services, the people join in a procession round the church. Sometimes, a real donkey leads the way!

On Palm Sunday, people who go to church are often given palm crosses—little crosses made out of palm leaves as a reminder both of that first Palm Sunday and of what was to happen on the Friday of that same week. Usually, the minister first says a prayer to bless the palm crosses before they are given to the people, or he may sprinkle them with "holy water" (which is water that has been blessed).

We call the day Palm Sunday because the people in Jerusalem greeted Jesus by waving palm branches. In Spain, it's called "Pascua Florida" which means "Flower Easter"—because flowers are often used to decorate the processions which take place there on this day. And, in turn, the Spanish name for this Sunday gave its name to the American state of Florida—because it was first discovered many years ago on "Pascua Florida" by people who came from Spain.

## WELCOMED AS A KING

Long, long ago, that first Palm Sunday was a very happy day indeed. Jesus rode into Jerusalem as a hero—even though he was seated on just a lowly donkey. The people of the city greeted him as a king, a man who would bring them freedom from the Roman army. Yet just a few days later, all those hopes and dreams seemed to be ended when he was put to death on the cross on what we now call Good Friday.

Brazilian children wait with patience and anticipation for their own Palm Sunday procession to begin.

But that Friday was not to be the end of the story. Three days later, Jesus was to come back to life again—and that is why, even today, people go to church on Palm Sunday to remember that first Palm Sunday procession with joy—and as a reminder that Jesus was to triumph over misery, suffering and hardship. Even though he rode into Jerusalem on just a "Palmesel" and despite what was to happen that first "Holy Week", he was still a great leader who would set his people free.

# 1 2

# *H O L Y   W E E K*

Palm Sunday was just the start of the week Jesus spent in Jerusalem. That week is now known as Holy Week and during these days (the last days of Lent) Christians remember how Jesus spent the last days of his earthly life. It was a week which began with him being very popular, cheered by the crowds as he rode into the city. It was to end very differently—with that same crowd shouting for him to be put to death by being nailed to a cross.

## PROCESSIONS AND PLAYS

During the three days following Palm Sunday, Jesus lived in a village near Jerusalem, called Bethany. He visited the city each day, teaching and talking to the people who gathered to hear him in the outer courtyard of the temple. Christians mark these days in different ways but many will go to church for special, solemn "Holy Week" services.

In some countries, such as Spain and Italy, there are processions through the streets. For example, during Holy Week in the Spanish city of Seville, there are processions every evening. Different groups of people take part, each carrying heavy platforms (called "pasos") on their shoulders. On these platforms are carvings showing scenes from that first Holy Week. Some of the wooden figures are dressed in elaborate clothes to show how important they are. The figure of Mary, the mother of Jesus, is often dressed as a queen and she is called the Queen of Pain—because of all the sorrow she must have suffered as she watched what happened to her son that week.

All of the platforms or "pasos" (there are more than a hundred!) are decorated with beautiful flowers and candles. They are followed in the procession by people dressed in white tunics and black hoods. These are "penitents", that is, people who are admitting how sorry they are for all the wrong things they have done.

On some "pasos", there are statues of Jesus on the cross, a scene called the Passion of Christ. "Passion" is a word often used to mean any strong feeling—such as love or anger. But the "Passion" of Jesus

means his suffering or agony.

In some towns at this time of year, people organize "Passion Plays". Not only do these plays tell about the events of Good Friday, but many of them also show what happened on the Thursday of the first Holy Week, Maundy Thursday.

In a small town in Guatemala, Christians walk in a procession to remind themselves (and everyone who sees them) of the events of the first Holy Week.

## JESUS' LAST MEAL

On the evening of this day, Jesus had a last meal, his Last Supper, with his twelve closest friends and followers—his disciples. By this stage of the week, many important people in Jerusalem had become angry at what Jesus had been teaching in the temple and so it was necessary that he and his disciples met secretly. This they did, in an upstairs room in the house of a friend—and it was here that he was to give them a special instruction or commandment. The Latin word for "commandment" is "mandatum" and it is from this word that the name "Maundy" comes.

But before giving them this commandment, Jesus washed the feet of his disciples. In a hot country (like Palestine) this was often done as a mark of respect to visitors and to make them comfortable after a long journey. It was a job done by servants or slaves—but Jesus himself did it as a way of showing he was humble and that following God often means serving others.

Since then, it has been a custom on Maundy Thursday for important people in the church to wash the feet of those in need. In Rome, the Pope washes the feet of twelve men (just as Jesus washed the feet of his twelve disciples). Other important church leaders, such as bishops, have also sometimes carried out this custom—as have some kings. This no longer happens in Great Britain (King James II was the last

This stained glass window in Lincoln Cathedral, England, shows Jesus washing his disciples' feet before their last meal together.

king to do this) but every Maundy Thursday the monarch goes to a service in a cathedral and gives out purses containing money to old people in need of help. The purses are given to as many old people as the age of the king or queen. So, when Queen Elizabeth was sixty, sixty old people were given "Maundy Money". In fact, they are each given two purses. In one are four specially minted silver coins; in the other purse is some ordinary money for them to use.

## SHARING AND CELEBRATING

But for most Christians, Maundy Thursday is remembered as the day of the Last Supper when Jesus gave his followers that special commandment. During the meal, he shared bread and wine with them and it

At the Last Supper Jesus shared bread and wine with his disciples as a way of showing that he was ready to give up his own life to save others from death.

was then he gave them the command-ment: "Do this in remembrance of me." (You can read about this in the Bible books of Matthew, chapter 26:26–28 and I Corinthians chapter 11:23–26.)

For most Christians, remembering or celebrating this Last Supper is a most important part of their faith. The service at which they do this is known by many names. Some people call it "communion" which means "sharing"; some call it the "Eucharist" (a Greek word meaning

"thanksgiving") and others call it the Lord's Supper, Breaking of Bread or Mass (see page 31).

Whatever it is called, Christians remember (and share in) this meal—especially on Sundays. But on Maundy Thursday evening, many of them will go to church to give thanks that Jesus gave them this commandment—because it is by sharing (by "holy communion") that they feel Jesus still helps them and gives them strength to live their daily lives.

# 13

# $G$OOD $FRIDAY$

It was on the Friday of Holy Week that the Jewish chief priests in Jerusalem sent Jesus for trial before the Roman governor whose name was Pontius Pilate. At first, Pilate could find nothing that Jesus had done wrong or which deserved the death penalty. But the chief priests had been encouraging the crowds of people to shout for Jesus to be put to death. In the end, Pilate gave way because he feared there might be a riot if he did not agree. So he sentenced Jesus to death—in the way that Romans always carried out executions. By crucifixion.

## FOLLOWING IN HIS FOOTSTEPS

Whenever anyone was condemned to death in the Roman Empire, he was made to walk through the city carrying a sign with both his name and his crime written on it. So, before his crucifixion, Jesus too had to walk to his place of execution carrying a sign. It read simply, "Jesus of Nazareth, King of the Jews"—for that is all that Pilate said should be written on Jesus' sign.

The route that some people believe Jesus had to take has since been walked by millions of Christians in memory of what happened to him that Friday. They follow the "Way of the Cross" through the narrow streets of the old part of the city. Along it are fourteen places where people stop to remember different things that happened to Jesus on *his* journey; these points are called "stations" or "the Stations of the Cross". Round the walls of churches all over the world are pictures or little statues which show what happened at each of these points. In some churches on Good Friday, there are processions in which people who can't visit Jerusalem may make their own "Way of the Cross".

## A WEARY WALK

The first "station" is the starting point: it's where the Roman fortress once stood, where Jesus was condemned to death. Nearby is the second station where he was given the heavy crossbeam to carry. (The upright post would already have been waiting for him at the place of execution.)

Those who follow the Way of the Cross must next make their way through the streets of the city, as Jesus had to that first Good Friday. They soon come to the third station which marks where he stumbled and fell for the first time under the weight of the cross. The fourth station is where, so it is said, he passed Mary his mother as she stood in the crowds on that terrible day. People following the Way of the Cross stop here, as they do at each station, to pray and think about how Jesus suffered.

## A HELPER IN THE CROWD

The next stopping point, the fifth, is where the Roman soldiers seized a man out of the crowd, a man called Simon from a place called Cyrene, and made him help Jesus carry the heavy beam.

The sixth station is where, so it is said, a woman wiped the sweat and blood from

In the time of Jesus the Temple stood on the oblong area, called Temple Mount, in the middle of Old Jerusalem. It was here that many of the events leading up to Good Friday took place.

Jesus' face. She's remembered today by the name Veronica, St Veronica.

The seventh station is where Jesus fell a second time, almost fainting from the effects of the heat and a beating he had been given earlier—and, of course, the weight of the cross.

Here the Way leads out of the old city, out through what were its boundary walls in the time of Jesus, to the eighth stopping point, where Jesus spoke to the women of Jerusalem. Next is the ninth station, where Jesus fell for a third time.

## THE CRUCIFIXION

The tenth stopping point is known as the Place of the Skull, Golgotha, where Jesus was to be crucified. This spot, and the remaining stations are now inside a great church, the Church of the Holy Sepulchre. At the tenth station, pilgrims remember how he was stripped of his clothes; and at the eleventh, how he was nailed to the

A modern Good Friday procession makes its way through the narrow streets of Old Jerusalem, just as Jesus must have done nearly two thousand years ago.

beam he'd been carrying and then hoisted up onto the cross.

At the twelfth station, they remember his death on the cross three hours later—and then they make their way to the thirteenth. Here they recall how his body was taken down from the cross and given to a man named Joseph from Arimathea and some friends of Jesus to put in a burial place. (You can read about this in the Bible book of Luke, chapter 23.) The last station marks that spot: the place where, it is said, the body of Jesus was laid to rest.

The Way of the Cross (or the "Via Dolorosa" as it's called in Latin) is a journey many pilgrims still make on their visits to Jerusalem. Some make it early in the morning, before the city is crowded with tourists and people going about their business. But every Friday, in the middle of the day, Franciscan friars lead a special commemoration of that first journey, made by Jesus on the Friday now called Good Friday—"good" because the Way of the Cross was not the end of the story.

Just outside the walls of Jerusalem there is a skull-like hill which still reminds people of "the Place of the Skull" where Jesus was crucified.

# 14

# *E* ASTER EVEN

Imagine you are in a little town on a Greek island such as Crete. It is the Saturday before Easter Day and everyone is very excited. Later, there will be fireworks—although the more impatient boys have

At midnight in some countries, Christians celebrate the resurrection of Jesus by setting off fireworks!

been setting light to theirs for several days now, frightening the older people of the town—and getting told off in return.

Even though it is late in the evening, the air is still warm and, in the moonlight, the white-painted stone church stands bright against the night sky. Outside the church, the young men have been building a huge bonfire. That's for later. Now, everyone is leaving their homes and the cafés and making their way to church. They each carry a candle—unlit, despite the fact it is already dark. Quickly the church becomes crowded and not everyone can get inside. Everyone stands as the lights are turned out and the Easter hymns are sung. Then comes the important part of the service. There is a procession and then the priest chants the story of the very first Easter: of how the friends of Jesus went to the cave where his body had been laid to rest after the crucifixion and how they found that he was no longer there.

And now it's almost midnight. The priest comes forward from the far end of the church carrying two lighted candles. "Come and take light," he says. The people nearest to him light their candles from the ones he is holding and then the other people light their candles in turn, one from another. The darkness gives way to light as more and more candles come to life in the little church. Soon the light is passed to those who were unable to get in and who are still outside.

And then it's midnight. The priest cries out the Easter greeting, "Christos anesti!" The Greek words mean "Christ is risen!" And the people shout the reply, "Alithos anesti!"—which means, "He is risen indeed!"

Then everyone hugs whoever they are standing next to, excited and happy as they exchange the Easter greeting. "Jesus Christ is risen." "He is risen indeed."

By now the bonfire has been lit and everyone comes out of church in great excitement. Fireworks are being set off and there is a great noise in the town square. The huge bonfire burns even more brightly as some of the younger men heave the trunk of an old tree on to it while the three bells of the church clang even more loudly as if to echo the excitement of the people.

As the night wears on there is singing and dancing but, gradually, different families begin to make their way home, carrying their candles with great care so that they don't blow out. Those who live farther away go home by car—with the children sitting in the back seat, doing their best to keep *their* candles alight. And then, once the candles are safely home, they are used to light all the oil lamps in the different homes.

So Christians in Greece begin their Easter celebration; Easter with its message

that, after the darkness and sorrow of Good Friday, come light and life and hope. For Christians believe that by dying on the cross Jesus made up for all our wrong-doing, so that it can now be forgiven. And by coming back to life he proved that his goodness can triumph over all evil.

People have celebrated the festival of Easter in similar ways in many other countries. Long, long ago in Britain, before there were handy things like boxes of matches and before there was any electricity, people used to go to church on Easter Even for "the new light". Before they went, as an act of faith, they would put out all their oil lamps and the fire in the hearth so that there was no fire or light at all in their home.

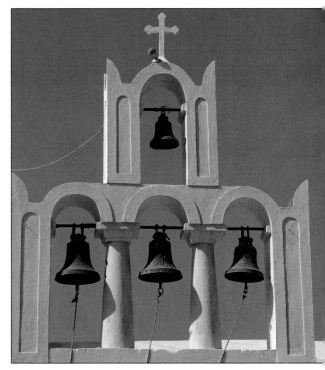

Church bells are rung to tell people that Easter Day has begun.

Crowds pack the cathedral at Zagorsk near Moscow to celebrate the most important festival of the Christian year.

Then, just like the people in Crete and other parts of Greece today, they made their way to church on the dark Saturday evening. And there, as part of the service, the priest would strike a stone or flint against the wall of the church until it made a spark from which a candle could be lit. And then, again just as in Greece today, the people would light their candles from that one candle. The priest would say, "Father, we share in the light of your glory, through your Son, the Light of the World. Make this new fire holy and inflame us with new hope." Then, after the service, the people would carry home the "new fire" of Easter, the light of life and hope. Only in Britain, you had to be extra careful that the blustery winds did not blow your candle out before you got home!

Services like this are still held in many Roman Catholic and some Anglican churches. Often, a very large candle is lit in the church and this is called the Paschal candle. "Paschal" is another word for Easter and most European names for Easter come from this word: for example, "Paques" (French), "Pascua" (Spanish), "Paach" (Dutch) and "Pask" (Swedish). And the Paschal candle is a symbol of Christ, the light of the world.

Traditionally the Paschal candle bears the Greek letters alpha and omega—the first and last letters of the Greek alphabet—to symbolize Christ, who was with God before the beginning of time and will return to earth at the end of the world.

# 15

# *E*ASTER DAY

Easter eggs, Easter chickens, Easter flowers . . . It's hard to imagine Easter happening at any time of the year except in spring. Unless of course you live in Australia, South Africa, or another country in the southern half of the world, and then you'll know it happens in the autumn. But wherever they live, people all around the world celebrate Easter in ways that remind them of springtime and of new life.

For Christians, the story goes back to the Sunday after Jesus was put to death on the cross and his body was laid in a tomb which was a bit like a cave that had a huge stone blocking its entrance.

## AN AMAZING SURPRISE

Very early that first Easter morning, one of Jesus' friends named Mary Magdalene went to the place where the tomb was. She was full of sorrow because she had seen Jesus die—but when she got to the tomb, she found the stone had been rolled away. And what is more, the tomb was empty!

She ran and told some other friends of Jesus and they came to see what had happened. Two of them, Peter and John, ran on ahead. John got to the tomb first but did

Chicks are popularly linked with Easter as a symbol of springtime and of new life.

not dare go inside. When Peter got there, they both went in. And yes, it *was* empty.

When Peter and John entered the garden tomb, all they found were empty graveclothes.

Later, they went away, wondering what it all meant. But Mary stayed there on her own, crying as she thought back to the crucifixion. After a while, a man spoke to her. "Why are you crying?"

"Because they have taken Jesus away and I don't know where they have laid him."

And then the man said, "Mary."

And she looked up and, through her tears, she recognized who it was. It was Jesus! He was alive! Jesus was no longer dead but alive! (You can read about this in the Bible book of John, chapter 20.)

And it is this "new life" that Christians celebrate on Easter Sunday morning—but what's it got to do with Easter eggs?

## SIGNS OF NEW LIFE

Even before the time of Jesus, people used to give each other eggs as a springtime gift, as a sign that new life was returning to the world after the cold, dead days of winter. In those days they didn't give chocolate eggs but real ones! For Christians however, the gift of an egg has an extra, special meaning. From the outside, an egg looks dead—like a stone. But inside, it contains a new life. So the shell is a bit like the tomb of Jesus; and, when this breaks, it is like the opening of the tomb and the beginning of a new life.

In Poland, at Easter, some people take a needle and make a tiny hole at each end of an egg. Then all the contents can be blown out. A pattern is made with wax on the outside of the empty shell. Next, the shell is dipped in bright dye—which stains the shell, except where the wax has been. This is done several times with different wax patterns and different dyes to make very attractive Easter presents.

In Germany (and in other countries) on

Easter Sunday morning, young children expect a visit from the Easter Hare—or "Oster Hase" as he's called in Germany. He's supposed to bring chocolate eggs and hide them in the garden, ready for children to find early on Easter morning.

Many different games are played with eggs at Easter. One game is played in much the same way, both in Greece and in parts of northern England. You hold an ordinary egg in your fist and knock it, end on, against your opponent's egg—to see whose is the stronger and whose egg can score most victories. The one thing you must remember before starting the game is that the eggs must be hard-boiled!

In lots of places, people play egg-rolling games at Easter. Again, hard-boiled eggs must be used! Often they are decorated with different colours and then rolled down hills to see whose egg can go the farthest before it breaks. They still play this game on the lawns of the White House in Washington D.C. where the president of the United States of America lives. This happens each year on Easter Monday when the gardens are open to the public.

So in many different ways, people have always celebrated springtime with its signs of new life, warmer days and the return of light to a world darkened during winter.

But for Christians, this great festival of

These Armenian Christians are on their way to an Easter service of celebration. For this festival, Christians from many countries like to visit Jerusalem—where the events of the first Easter took place.

**The Garden Tomb in Jerusalem reminds visitors today of the empty tomb.**

Easter is far more than a celebration of springtime. It is a reminder of the return to life of Jesus after his death on the cross. What's more, it is the day of the year (more than any other) when Christians remember how, by rising from the dead, Jesus showed that there was a new life after death—for everyone. By his suffering and dying on the cross (so Christians believe), Jesus has made it possible for us all to share in that new life. No wonder then that, for Christians, Easter Day is a very special celebration—and the most important festival of the year!

# 16

# ASCENSION DAY

On Good Friday, Jesus died on the cross. A horrible death. On Easter Sunday, he came back to life. Gloriously, wondrously. And during the forty days which followed that first Easter, he kept appearing to his followers. In some ways he seemed different. Two of his friends spent some time talking to him as they walked along a road—without recognizing him. But at other times, he appeared to his followers and they knew exactly who he was. Jesus of Nazareth who was dead and was now alive again.

Of that they were certain. That he was alive, real. Real enough to touch. No wonder Christians remember those forty days following Easter as the Forty Glorious Days.

## A WONDERFUL PROMISE

But they were to come to an end. On the day we now call Ascension Day (it's always a Thursday—forty days after Easter Sunday), Jesus led his closest friends to the top of a small hill just outside the city of Jerusalem. When they got there, he repeated a promise he had made before he

was crucified. It was that he would not leave them alone but that the Holy Spirit would come to them and be with them always. Then Jesus told them that they must travel the world, telling everyone about him, about what he had done and what he had taught.

When he had finished speaking, a low cloud covered the hilltop and hid him from them. And when the cloud lifted, he was gone. They stood there, staring. Where was Jesus?

Then two men, dressed in white, whom they had never seen before, appeared and spoke to them. "What are you doing? Why are you staring up into the sky like that? Jesus is now in heaven." (You can read about this in the Bible book of Acts, chapter 1.)

## A DAY TO CELEBRATE

Ascension Day might seem to be a sad day: the end of the life of Jesus on earth. It's not. It's the very opposite: it's a glorious festival, a day to celebrate. For Jesus had now

"As Jesus blessed his disciples, he was taken up into heaven." This ancient stained glass window in Ulm Cathedral, Germany, shows what might have happened on the first Ascension Day.

finished his work in earth and had returned home to God, his Father in heaven. What is more, his disciples now understood many of the things he had told them earlier. That they must continue the work he had been doing on earth. That one day, they too would be with him in heaven. And this is what all Christians believe: that they must try to live their lives as Jesus wants them to do—and that, one day, they will be with him in heaven.

The word "Ascension" means "going up"—and the day is called this because the cloud that hid Jesus from his disciples seemed to carry him upwards into heaven.

It is one of the most important days of the church's year, after Christmas and Easter. In many countries, it's a holiday. In others (including Britain) people no longer take as much notice of it as they once did. But in olden times, all the churches would be crowded for Ascension Day services and, sometimes, a statue of Jesus or a "crucifix" (that is, a large cross with the figure of Jesus on it) would be lifted high above the heads of the people. In some places, it was actually hauled right up through a hole in the church roof and out of sight. Not a bad way of showing people what happened the very first Ascension Day!

A decorated or "dressed" well at Youlgreave in Derbyshire, England. Made mainly from flower petals pressed into clay, this is a picture of the Last Supper.

## MAKING THE DAY SPECIAL

Another custom that sometimes took place on Ascension Day was "Beating the Bounds". This was a way of fixing in everyone's mind exactly where one village (or parish) began and ended: a way of marking its "bounds" or boundaries.

The priest and all the important people in the local church would get all the children of the village together and march them off in a procession round its boundary. They stopped wherever there was a landmark such as a tree or big stone. There, one of the boys of the village would be beaten with sticks from a willow tree! If there was a pond or stream beside the boundary, then a boy would be ducked in the water! It was done in a teasing kind of way but it could still be rather cold! One thing was certain, after you had been made to take part in "beating the bounds", you never forgot where the edge of your village was! Fortunately this no longer happens!

Another ancient British custom that took place at this time of the year (and still does in some northern villages) is "well dressing".

Water is of course something we cannot do without and a spring or well which provides clean, cool water was *very* precious in the days before taps and piped water. So, as a way of giving thanks for this supply of fresh water, people "dressed" or decorated these springs and wells in springtime. This happened long before Christianity arrived in Britain. Later, it became a thanksgiving to God at Ascension time for the gift of water.

A board would be covered in clay and then an arrangement of flowers, moss, shells, twigs and fir cones would be pressed into the clay to make a bright and cheerful picture. Nothing artificial or machine-made was ever used in the pictures (or "collages") and the clay was watered to keep the flowers fresh for several days.

In other places, well dressing takes place on the next festival of the year: Pentecost. That is the day on which a promise made by Jesus to his disciples would come true, the promise that the Holy Spirit would come to them. (You can read about this in the Bible book of John, chapter 14:26.)

# 17

# *PENTECOST (OR WHITSUN)*

At this time of the year in some towns in the north of England, people take part in Whit Walks. At the head of each of these processions is a band. Then come children from the different churches and Sunday schools in the area, some carrying banners showing the name of their church. After them come their parents and other grown-ups. The biggest of these cheerful processions used to be held in Manchester. Those who still take part in these walks do so to "witness" or to show everyone else that their Christian faith is important to them; it's not something to be kept secret.

The name "Whitsun" comes from a much older name: White Sunday. In the

past, this was the day of the year on which people were baptized (or made members of the church) and, as they usually wore white clothes on this day, that is probably how the day got its name. But it is also linked with red and with fire.

## WIND AND FIRE

In most countries, this Sunday is known as Pentecost. The name "Pentecost" comes from a Greek word which means "fiftieth"— and Pentecost Sunday (or Whitsun) is fifty days after Easter (which means it is ten days after Ascension Day).

On that very first Pentecost Sunday, the followers of Jesus had met together in an upstairs room in Jerusalem. (Perhaps it was the same one in which they had shared their Last Supper with Jesus.) As they were praying together, there suddenly came a sound like a powerful wind. It seemed as if the wind were rushing through the house and, as the disciples looked at each other, there seemed to be tongues of fire on each of their heads—but they were not harmed in any way. Then they realized that, as he promised, Jesus was sending his Holy Spirit to be with them, to be *in* them, as a source of strength and courage as they carried on his work. And the tongues of fire were indeed signs of the Holy Spirit. And it is because of the fire that red is the colour of Pentecost.

*Opposite.* "Whit Walks" have taken place in some English towns for many years. This one (in Manchester at around the turn of the century) shows all the girls dressed traditionally in white.

## GOOD NEWS FOR EVERYONE

The disciples then remembered what Jesus had told them they must do. Straightaway, they went out into the streets of the city

**"Filled with the Holy Spirit" at Pentecost, Peter and the other disciples were able to speak confidently about their faith in the risen Jesus.**

and began telling everyone what he had taught them: how he had been crucified on the cross, how he had risen from the dead and how he had brought good news for all people and the promise of a life in heaven after this one on earth.

Because that day was a holiday, Jerusalem was very crowded with visitors from many countries. At first these people thought that Peter and the other disciples of Jesus must be drunk as they seemed so excited and talkative. Peter convinced them that they weren't drunk and carried on telling the crowds about Jesus. And the extraordinary thing was, whichever country the people came from, they understood what the disciples were saying as if they were hearing their own language.

Since the baptism of Jesus, the dove has been a symbol of the Holy Spirit.

On that day, three thousand people became followers of Jesus. As this was really the start of the Christian church, it makes Pentecost the "birthday" of the church.

## A SPECIAL HELPER

At Pentecost, the disciples and the others who had become Christians said they were "filled with the Holy Spirit"—meaning that they felt God was very close to them, actually in them; guiding them and helping them in what they had to do. Christians today also believe that the Holy Spirit is with them, helping them. Some believe this

happens especially at holy communion when they eat the bread and wine in memory of Jesus (as he told his followers to do at his Last Supper).

Other Christians believe the Holy Spirit comes to them in a special way at any time they meet together. Sometimes they start talking in languages (or "tongues") like no known languages in the world. This is called "speaking in tongues". Other people who are present may feel the Holy Spirit is helping them to "translate" what these people are saying.

## DOVES AND TRUMPETS

Pentecost (or Whitsun) has been celebrated in all sorts of ways. In some churches, a white dove used to be set free

as a sign that the Holy Spirit was present. Even now (and especially in churches in Eastern Europe) you can see paintings of a dove—as a reminder that the Holy Spirit is present at all times. The reason a painting of a dove is chosen to represent the Holy Spirit is because, when Jesus was baptized (see page 12), he felt the Holy Spirit come to him "like a dove" from heaven. (You can read about this in the Bible book of Matthew, chapter 3.)

In France they sometimes blow trumpets in church as a reminder of the mighty wind that blew through the house where the disciples were. Others fly kites as a reminder of that same wind. And at a village called El Rocio in Spain a statue of Mary, the mother of Jesus, and the baby Jesus is carried in a huge procession.

Christians pray "to God the Father, God the Son and God the Holy Spirit". This does not mean they have three gods. They believe there is one God: God the Father who has existed always; God who also came to earth as Jesus and is called the Son of God; and God the Holy Spirit who is present with them—helping, strengthening and comforting them at all times.

# 18

# *C ORPUS CHRISTI*

A day for watching plays—that's what Corpus Christi used to be for many people. But what's the meaning of this festival with an odd name?

Just as Pentecost comes ten days after the Ascension, so Corpus Christi comes ten days after Pentecost. Corpus Christi is little-known in mainly Protestant countries, but for several hundred years it has been an important festival in the Roman Catholic Church. Its name is Latin for "the body of Christ".

## GIVING THANKS

It was first celebrated in the year 1264. People thought there should be a special day of the year on which to say "thank you" to God for his gift of holy communion, the church service at which Christians believe God comes to them in a special way through bread and wine. Many Christians feel the right time to give thanks for holy communion is on the evening of Maundy Thursday (the night when Jesus had his Last Supper with his disciples). But there are those who feel that because Maundy

Thursday is in Lent and so close to Good Friday, that is not a good time of year for a cheerful celebration. So the feast or festival of Corpus Christi came to be celebrated on a Thursday in late May or early June (its exact date depends on the date of Easter).

## PLAYS WITH A MESSAGE . . .

In England, within a few years of its starting, it had become a very special kind of holiday: a day for watching religious plays acted in the streets of the big cities. In some places, you could see as many as thirty plays in one day! Each of them was rehearsed and acted by a group of people who all worked at the same job. For example: bakers, carpenters or water carriers (men who delivered buckets of water to each house). Each play (or "pageant") told a story from the Bible. They were performed on special carts which could be wheeled from one stopping place to another, round the town—and the play was performed at each stop. So if you had come into the city to see

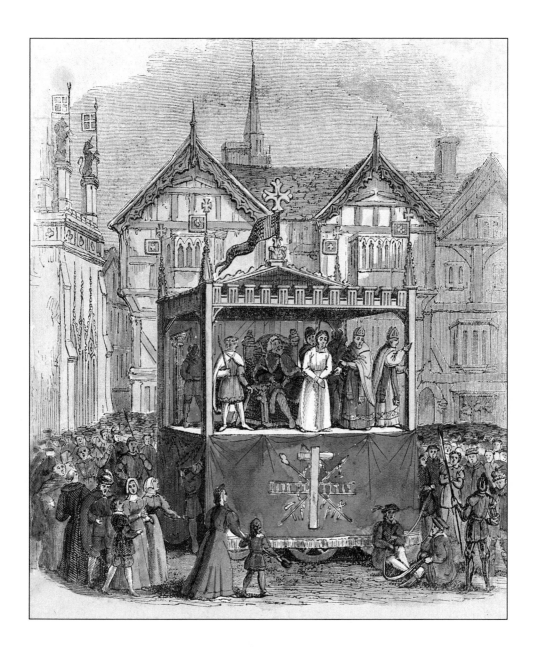

This old engraving shows how a special cart was used as the stage for religious plays in medieval times.

the plays, you would choose a good place to stand, early in the day, and then each play (on its own wagon) would come along, stop—and you could watch the play. It was the job of a man called the pageant master to make sure the wagons (and plays) arrived in the right order!

In those days, very few people could read or write. What is more, the Bible was written only in Latin so most of the people could not understand it even when it was read aloud in the church. So these plays were a good way of teaching the people the stories told in the Bible.

Everyone wears their very best (traditional) clothes when they take part in this Corpus Christi procession in Poland.

### ... AND WITH FUN!

But many of the plays had comic scenes added that weren't in the Bible! For example, at the town of Wakefield in Yorkshire, there was a play about the first Christmas Eve which told how the shepherds on the hillside near Bethlehem went to visit the baby Jesus. Besides telling that story, it has a lot of jokes about a shepherd called Mak (never mentioned in the Bible!) who tries to steal a young sheep that belongs to one of the other shepherds.

He takes it home and, when the other shepherds come looking for it, he hides it in a baby's cradle and pretends his wife has just had a baby. Then the sheep starts

bleating! "I pray you, go home," says Mak.

"Let me lift up the cloth and give your baby a kiss," says one of the shepherds.

Mak tries to stop him—but without any luck. He is found out and, as a punishment, is tossed up and down in the air in a blanket—and then all the shepherds in the play take presents to the baby Jesus.

We do not know for sure which group of workers acted this play at Wakefield but a similar one at Coventry was acted by the sheep-shearers and tailors. Indeed, all the plays were acted by people whose job had some connection with the story told in that play. So, at Chester, the water-carriers acted the story of Noah and the Flood. In York, the nail-makers performed the story of the crucifixion and the bakers acted the story especially connected with the festival of Corpus Christi: the Last Supper.

There are processions and celebrations in other countries at this time of the year. In Italy, "Corpus Domini" (which means "the body of the Lord") is a great festival held one Sunday in June. At Genzano di Roma (a town near Rome) there is a famous "Infiorata" or flower festival when a huge carpet of flowers is created in the town.

Corpus Christi is the last of the big festivals of the church's year, festivals which tell the story of Jesus from Advent (which looks forward to his coming) and Christmas (when he was born) to his crucifixion, rising to life again and Ascension. Then come Whitsun (or Pentecost) and Corpus Christi which are reminders that, although Jesus went back to be with God in heaven, God is still with those who follow the way taught by Jesus.

A thief tries to disguise a stolen lamb as a baby in one traditional religious play.

# 19

# *HARVEST AND THANKSGIVING*

Suppose you were to go into your nearest supermarket or the shop where you buy your food—and find that all of the shelves were empty. "What's happened?" you ask the man who works there. "Why is there no food?"

"Oh, it wasn't a very good harvest," he replies. "We won't have much food till next year."

Nowadays, most of us are used to being able to go to the shops to buy all the food we want any time of the year. We have become so used to having canned or frozen food, we expect there always to be plenty—however good or bad the last harvest was.

But if you live in the country or in an area that grows its own food, you'll know just how important harvest is. Harvest: the time of the year when all the crops are gathered in. The grain is cut to make flour and then bread. Vegetables are picked ready for eating (or freezing or putting into cans)—and all the fruit has ripened.

Not all that long ago, before there were fridges and freezers and cans that keep food safe for many months, it mattered a

lot whether it was a good harvest each autumn. A poor harvest meant going hungry during the winter (as it still does in many countries). A good harvest was something to be really grateful for. No wonder then that people have wanted to thank God for all his gifts of food at harvest time; no wonder that, each autumn, churches hold Harvest Festivals, especially in country villages.

### THANKS FOR THE HARVEST

Just before Harvest Festival, the villagers spend a lot of time decorating their church. Apples are arranged along all the window sills and bunches of grapes are hung from all sorts of unlikely places! Heaps of vegetables are arranged along the steps and bunches of wheat or barley are made to stand by the seats for the choir. There are also displays of specially-made loaves, trays of eggs and bunches of flowers. Each of them has been brought by different families from their gardens or farms as a "thank you" to God for the food that has

People may gather wild fruits or cultivated crops at harvest time. Crops vary from country to country, but wherever you live, a good harvest means plenty of food for everyone.

grown during the summer and which will keep everyone fed during the coming winter.

Then, when they go to church on Sunday morning, it's like going into a splendid market hall! And everyone sings popular harvest hymns such as:

*Come ye thankful people, come,*
*Raise the song of Harvest-home:*
*All is safely gathered in,*
*Ere the winter storms begin;*
*God, our Maker, doth provide*
*For our wants to be supplied.*

After the service, the food is sometimes sold, and the money given to really needy people in other countries, and the flowers sent to people in hospital.

At harvest time in some parts of Austria, carriages are decorated with flowers—and people ride to church in style.

In olden days, "Harvest-home" was the most important part of the harvest. This was a great feast or harvest supper. It was held after the last field had been harvested and when all was "safely gathered in". In those days (before there were big farm machines like combine harvesters) harvesting was a long and tiring job. So it was a great relief when the job was finished and everyone could relax. For many of the farmworkers, the harvest-home was the biggest and best meal of the year—until Christmas, at least.

The idea of celebrating harvest goes back much further than the time of Jesus—and you don't have to be a Christian to be grateful for harvest. So Harvest is not a specially Christian festival in the way that Christmas and Easter are. But Christians, like other people, have wanted to say thank you at this time of the year for what they have been given.

So, long ago, they began to hold a feast at the *start* of the harvest. When the first wheat had been cut, it was made into special little loaves. These were taken to church and used at a holy communion service on the first day of August. This was called "loaf-mass" but later it was shortened to "Lammas". It is still known as Lammas Day in some parts of Great Britain but Lammas services are now held in only a very few churches.

However, in the year 1843 a clergyman named the Reverend R. S. Hawker, living in south-west England, started the idea of holding harvest festivals at the *end* of the harvest. Christians still do this—and not just in country churches but in town and city ones as well. In some seaside churches, fishermen bring some of the fish they have caught to be part of the thanksgiving. In others, coal miners even offer coal they have dug from deep in the earth. For the important thing about Harvest is saying "thank you" to God—for *all* his gifts.

## THANKSGIVING

In North America, a similar celebration took place in the autumn of 1621 when the pilgrims who had crossed from Europe gathered their first harvest. This celebration became a popular custom and, in 1798, President George Washington said that one day each year should be officially kept as "Thanksgiving Day". It is now celebrated on the fourth Thursday in November in the USA and is a national holiday. Canadians celebrate Thanksgiving on the second Monday in October.

Today, like Harvest, Thanksgiving is seen by many people as a day on which to thank God for all the good things of life.

A loaf of bread shaped like a sheaf of corn will often be baked as a church decoration at harvest time.

# 20

# *H*ALLOWTIDE

The last day of October is known as Hallowe'en in Britain, but it may also be called "Trick or Treat" in the United States of America. In either case, the evening of this day is a very spooky time! A night for mischief, witches and ghosts! Or at least, that's what some people think it is . . .

In America, children go from house to house saying, "Trick or treat?" The people in each house can then decide either to give their young visitors a "treat" (most often something sweet to eat or some money) or they can say no. But then they must be prepared for a "trick". For, if the young people calling on them don't get a "treat", they will feel free to play a trick on that house—like emptying their rubbish bins over the path or rubbing soap on a window!

In some countries, Hallowe'en is a time for playing games like bobbing for apples. To do this, you have to see how many apples you can get out of a deep bowl of water. The apples float on the water—so it sounds easy.

Except that you can't use your hands and must use only your mouth. You end up getting your face (and head) very wet indeed!

Hallowe'en is also a time when some people think witches and ghosts are about, ready to cause trouble. To scare them away, people make lanterns out of turnips or pumpkins. The turnip or pumpkin is hollowed out and slits are cut in it, like a nose and mouth and eyes. Then a candle is placed inside it, lighting it up like a grinning, ghostly face.

In Central America, 2 November is the Day of the Dead. People may visit family graves and decorate them elaborately—like this one in Zunil Cemetery, Guatemala. It is not a gloomy day, but a festival when people remember the happy times they have spent with friends and relations who are now dead.

## GOOD IS STRONGER THAN EVIL

This idea of Hallowe'en goes back to long before people became Christians. In those days they thought that, as the nights got darker and longer, evil and wickedness got stronger. But those who believe in God know that goodness cannot be defeated by evil and that all the frightening things about Hallowe'en are overcome by Jesus' victory over death, which is remembered on the next two days of the year, a time called Hallowtide.

"Hallow" is a word meaning to "make holy". So Hallowe'en (or All Hallows' Evening) is the night before a day when goodness and holiness win a victory over everything that is bad or evil. Although this time is not celebrated widely or even in every country, the first day of November (All Saints' Day) is an important festival of the Christian year.

An especially good or holy person is called a "saint" and each saint is remembered on one particular day of the year. So, for example, the disciple Peter (now called St Peter) is remembered on 29 June. Another disciple, St John, is remembered on 27 December. St Joseph, the husband of Mary the mother of Jesus, has his saint's day on 19 March. But all the unknown, forgotten or unrecognized saints have their special day at the very start of November: All Saints' Day.

"Soul cakes"—once a traditional food for the eve of All Souls' Day.

## REMEMBERING THE DEAD

The next day of the year, 2 November, is All Souls' Day. In some places it's called the Day of the Dead or "Deads' Day". This is because it is time for remembering not just good people who have died but *everyone* who has died—good or bad. Some families make a point of visiting graveyards or cemeteries and putting flowers on the graves of members of their family who are buried there. This may seem a rather sad thing to do. It's not. It's a time to remember the good and happy times they had when they were alive; and a time for their families to say prayers that their souls may now be at peace and enjoying all the joy of heaven that Jesus promised.

In olden times, it was believed that dead people came back to earth on All Souls' Day to taste ordinary food again. So there was a custom in some places of preparing a meal the night before All Souls' Day (that is, on the evening of All Saints' Day) and leaving it ready for the dead to come and eat late at night! The meal was usually a glass of wine and little cakes which were called "soul cakes".

Of course, this was all only a story and so, over the years, the custom was changed. Instead, the soul cakes were given to poor people. Sometimes, people would go "souling". A group would get together and visit all the big houses in the area, singing a song which asked for soul cakes:

*Soul, soul, for a soul cake!*
*I pray, good mistress, for a soul cake!*

So the Christian year ends with everyone thinking about death! It might seem a little gloomy to end this way but for Christians, death *isn't* the end of everything. It's a new beginning—of a life in heaven. And in the same way, Hallowtide isn't the end of everything. In less than a month, it'll be Advent and time to look forward to the beginning of a new year and the birth of Jesus at Christmas!

# INDEX

# INDEX